RAISING CHILDREN IN ISLAM

Published by Al-Quran Society
London, United Kingdom

Cover art and typesetting by Ihsaan Design
www.ihsaandesign.com

RAISING CHILDREN IN ISLAM

Suhaib Hasan

Al-Quran Society   جَمْعِيَّـة القُـُرْآن

CONTENTS

PREAMBLE

This book is based not only on years of specialised study in this field but also reflects my own personal experiences in a family filled with children over 30 years of married life. I was brought up in a conservative and deeply religious family in the Indian subcontinent. I had my own turbulent experiences of helping my wife raise our own six children, initially in a simple Asian/African community in Kenya, and later in the complex multicultural environment of Britain.

Through the progress of my progeny from school to university, I learned of the British educational system, from the egalitarian approach of modern comprehensive schools, an idealistic concept often defeated by lack of funding, to the elitist and successful private sector which insists on rigorous discipline, tradition and high academic achievement.

Life in Britain opens the door to a myriad of contrasts in value systems, customs, races and beliefs. The Muslim discovers that his Islamic values and faith are not only alien to the dominant western culture throughout the society, but that the two insist on locking horns in battle. This struggle of two opposing yet equally dogmatic belief systems engulfs and threatens to drown the Muslims. Some fortunate ones swim through the ocean of parenthood with smiling faces, having successfully negotiated the obstacles thrown their way.

They smile because not only have they survived the test with their own faith and values intact, but have also succeeded in transmitting their beliefs and norms to their children. Imagine the content and sense of achievement parents must feel when observing their adult children who too share the same love and devotion to the Mosque, the Quran and the many Islamic precepts. In a world obsessed with materialism and denial of God, this is truly a great achievement.

Unhappily there are many more parents who flounder and sink, who do not share this sense of achievement and jubilation, and who weep with sorrow and failure when observing their own offspring: aged parents confronted with the dreadful spectacle of their indecently dressed daughter going to the pub with her arms around her current boyfriend, or their beloved son who buys the attentions of street women and even fathers illegitimate children. These parents feel as if the earth is dropping from under their feet and they are being swallowed by quicksand, powerless and helpless. They wish they could have a second chance at raising their children but there is never a second chance.

This small booklet is presented to those young men and women beginning the long journey of parenthood, in the hope that they may never shed the tears of the defeated.

Suhaib Hasan
September 1997
London

CHAPTER ONE

<u>YOUTH CULTURE TODAY</u>

The family is the basic nucleus and core of society. The state of family life determines the health of the nation. A healthy society requires that its individuals know morals, socially acceptable codes of behaviour, respect for others, care of the weak and disadvantaged, consideration for the property of others, value for hard work, and much more.

The Muslim will add much more to the above list, including fear of Allah in all matters, love and obedience to Him before obedience to any creation, the desire to earn paradise taking priority over the desire to succeed in this world, and the importance of keeping to Halal and avoiding Haram.

All these values and morals are crucial for any decent society, but they cannot be learned from books or occasional lectures. They need to be inculcated in all individuals from a young age so that as they grow older and temptations cross their paths, which they inevitably must in the life of every individual, they will be able to avoid them. If good values and beliefs are deeply entrenched in the minds of individuals from childhood, they will remain with them throughout their lives.

If children are taught no guiding principles, they will in all probability wander aimlessly through life, looking for cheap and short-lived thrills, like fireworks which explode with huge bangs and rainbows of colours, but are immediately silent for ever. The bored and aimless youth who frequent pubs, pop concerts and all-night raves, poisoning their bodies with drugs, cigarettes and alcohol, are living in a world of fireworks. Their addictions are expensive, give thrills for a short time and then disappear, leaving a void which needs more money and more drugs to fill it again temporarily.

This may seem a harsh appraisal of the youth culture which exists around us today, but who can doubt its validity and truth? And more tragically, are not our Muslim youth trapped in the same vicious circle as a result of boredom, unemployment, purposeless lives, little parental guidance and neither fear nor love of The Almighty?

Muslim parents from all backgrounds have become adept at blaming everyone except themselves for the wrongdoings of their unruly offspring. Teachers are blamed for not handling their violent or disruptive pupils properly. Governments are blamed for not providing employment, training and better prospects. Local councils are blamed for not providing leisure activities for the youth. And the non-Muslim West is blamed for leading the youth away from Islam. In despair the elderly parents of wayward sons and daughters will often pack their bags and tearfully return "home". Little do they realise that the problem lies in themselves and their upbringing of their children, and from this there can be no running away.

Parents need to stop hunting for scapegoats for the shameful behaviour of their children, and instead examine themselves and their relationships with their children. How many parents can claim to be able to communicate with their children? They may talk to each other, but are they communicating with and understanding each other? Sadly, many Muslim youth today feel they have no close relationship with their parents and are unable to confide in them. Their mothers see their role as providing food, clean laundry, nursing during illness, a tidy home, but little more. The fathers see their duty as providing an income and a roof over their heads, but they spend as little leisure time with their children.

Consequently a gulf appears between these two generations, becoming insurmountable as the children grow older. The youth are thus forced to look outside the home for support, friendship, advice and role-models. Returning home from school, they have no choice but to devise their own entertainment, whether it be playing in the streets until darkness, or watching anything and everything on television. The parents may be providing for the physical health of their children, but spiritual, educational and emotional support is equally important and must not be ignored.

THE ISLAMIC PERSPECTIVE

The Quran has placed immense emphasis on the role of parents in bringing up their children in a good Islamic environment. In fact, Allah Almighty has made this an obligation upon parents and guardians:

يَـٰٓأَيُّهَا ٱلَّذِينَ ءَامَنُوا۟ قُوٓا۟ أَنفُسَكُمْ وَأَهْلِيكُمْ نَارًا وَقُودُهَا ٱلنَّاسُ وَٱلْحِجَارَةُ

O you who believe! Save yourselves and your families from a Fire, the fuel of which is humans and stones... (*Sūrah at-Taḥrīm,* 66:6)

The first stage of fulfilling this commandment is that each individual must save his own soul from the fires of Hell. It is a sad reality that human beings fear the tiny flames of matches, taking many kinds of precautions against fires in their own homes; fire alarms are installed to detect the first signs of smoke, smoke-retardant furniture is purchased, and fireguards are fitted. And if a person's house was to catch fire, he would be quick to save himself and his family, giving no second thought to his valuables burning inside.

But the folly of man is such that he has forgotten the ultimate Fire which awaits him. The Quran has described vividly the leaping flames of Hell which are 70 times hotter than the most dreadful infernos of earth. This fire is burning and eagerly awaits its occupants, while much of mankind is on a train speeding directly towards it. Man is aware that life on earth is temporary, he is aware that the flames of Hell are awaiting him, but he refuses to alter the direction of his life in any way.

The people with sense are not oblivious to the dangers waiting and have chosen to direct their efforts towards Paradise, also described vividly in the Qur'an. No man would run from his blazing house, happy to have saved his own skin, if his family members were still trapped in the house. Similarly, no man should relish the prospect of enjoying the luxuries of Paradise while his loved ones burn in Hell. It thus makes sense for every individual to strive for heaven and ensure that his friends and family also do the same. The first step would be for each individual to choose a marriage partner who will aid and not hinder his or her efforts to enter Paradise. Secondly, they will need to raise their children in Islam so that they too will enter Jannah with their parents. Allah Almighty has promised to keep such righteous families together in Paradise, provided that each one of them has individually earned the right to enter it:

جَنَّٰتُ عَدْنٍ يَدْخُلُونَهَا وَمَن صَلَحَ مِنْ ءَابَآئِهِمْ وَأَزْوَٰجِهِمْ وَذُرِّيَّٰتِهِمْ ۖ وَٱلْمَلَٰٓئِكَةُ يَدْخُلُونَ عَلَيْهِم مِّن كُلِّ بَابٍ ۞ سَلَٰمٌ عَلَيْكُم بِمَا صَبَرْتُمْ ۚ فَنِعْمَ عُقْبَى ٱلدَّارِ

Eternal Gardens they shall enter, and also those who acted righteously from among their fathers, their wives and their children. And angels shall enter unto them from every gate, saying, "Peace be upon you, for your perseverance in patience." Wonderful indeed is the final home. (*Sūrah ar-Ra'd*, 13:23-24)

Even the angels who carry the Throne of Allah and stand next to it make the same prayer for the believers and their families:

رَبَّنَا وَأَدْخِلْهُمْ جَنَّٰتِ عَدْنٍ ٱلَّتِي وَعَدتَّهُمْ وَمَن صَلَحَ مِنْ ءَابَآئِهِمْ وَأَزْوَٰجِهِمْ وَذُرِّيَّٰتِهِمْ ۚ إِنَّكَ أَنتَ ٱلْعَزِيزُ ٱلْحَكِيمُ

**Our Lord! Make them enter the Eternal Gardens which
You have promised them, and to the righteous among
their fathers, their wives, and their offspring. Verily
You are the All-Mighty, All-Wise. (*Sūrah Ghāfir*, 40:8)**

The believer is always conscious of his duty to save himself and his
family from the Hell-fire. He remembers the Prophet's ﷺ words,
*"Every one of you is a shepherd, and every one of you is responsible for
his flock."* (Bukhari, Muslim & Tirmidhi)

Bearing this in mind, marriage and parenthood are huge
responsibilities, not just for a few years but for a whole lifetime. Any
men or women contemplating marriage need to be aware of their
duties and of the Islamic guidelines laid down to help make their task
easier.

CHAPTER TWO

<u>BEFORE MARRIAGE</u>

The subject of finding, suitable spouses for young men and women continues to cause grievance and debate within the Muslim community. Ideally, the parents of the individual will take this huge task on their own shoulders and will search for a compatible spouse for their son or daughter. Unfortunately, this is often an unobtainable dream for many youngsters whose hopes and aspirations are not always matched by those of their elders. Tribal loyalties, family customs and an obsession with cousin-marriages can leave the youngsters and their elders tugging in opposite directions, often with miserable consequences.

The first advice for anyone looking to get married is to pray to Allah Almighty to fulfil one's dreams. One of the best supplications for this is found in the Qur'an:

$$
\text{وَمِنْهُم مَّن يَقُولُ رَبَّنَآ ءَاتِنَا فِى ٱلدُّنْيَا حَسَنَةً وَفِى ٱلْأَخِرَةِ حَسَنَةً}
$$

$$
\text{وَقِنَا عَذَابَ ٱلنَّارِ}
$$

Our Lord! Grant us good in this world, and good in the Hereafter, and save us from the punishment of the Fire.
(*Sūrah al-Baqarah*, 2:201)

"Good in this world" can mean many different things, but especially a pious husband or wife. When looking for a bride, a young man and his family should remember the following advice given by the Prophet ﷺ to his Companions,

14

A woman is married for four things: her wealth, her beauty, her lineage or her piety. Always choose a woman who is pious in the practice of her religion. (Bukhārī, Muslim. Abū Dāwūd & Nasā'ī)

Wealth will pass and will not always remain in one's hands. Beauty will fade away, and lineage has no value with Allah. Remember:

$$ إِنَّ أَكْرَمَكُمْ عِندَ ٱللَّهِ أَتْقَلْكُمْ $$

The most noble among you before Allah are the most pious. (*Sūrah al-Ḥujurāt,* 49:13)

Islam places no value on the colour of a person's skin, their financial status, lineage or rank in society. The only enduring thing of value is Taqwa (piety and fear of Allah). The Prophet ﷺ once extolled the virtues of pious wives with the following words,

A believer cannot earn for himself after the Fear of Allah, anything better than a pious wife. She obeys him when he commands her, she is pleasing to him when he looks at her, if he takes an oath from her to do something she does it, she preserves her chastity and guards his wealth when he is absent. (Ibn Majah)

TO SEE OR NOT TO SEE

Muslims seem to enjoy going to extremes where their religion is concerned, instead of following the middle and recommended path. This is especially true in marriage where Islam permits prospective spouses to see each other once for a formal conversation and in the presence of a chaperone. A Companion once approached the Prophet ﷺ and expressed his intention to marry a girl from the people of Ansar in Madinah. The Prophet advised him to see the girl, saying that some Anṣārī women were known to have defects in their eyes (Aḥmad & Nasā'ī). In another narration, the Prophet ﷺ advised his companions to see their prospective partners because this would put love between their hearts.

Yet some Muslim communities go to one extreme and forbid categorically any meetings between the couple, so that often the first time they see each other is at their wedding. Some couples may accept this, but an increasing number of young people do not wish to enter married life clueless about their spouses.

The other extreme is that of Muslims who use the Ḥadīth permitting the couple to see each other to allow a number of increasingly informal meetings. Courtship is not permitted in Islam, and any information the couple require about each other should be obtained through family and friends. The Prophet ﷺ has forbidden men and women who are not Maḥrams (closely-related) from sitting together in privacy by saying, *"Whenever a man sits with a woman in privacy, a third one always creeps in, and that is Satan"* (Tirmidhī). An engaged couple do not fall under the category of Maḥrams.

Yet we hear of Muslim youth clamouring for clubs where matrimonially-inclined men and women can meet and find partners. The exponents of this idea assure us that all participants will be dressed modestly and any conversations between opposite sexes will be very formal and proper. If the farce of such clubs were to be introduced, it would only encourage laxity of morals and conduct within the Muslim community. Islamic guidelines on contact between the sexes are detailed and strict, as it is only with such firm codes that a decent and moral society can be created. Once we begin to abandon any of these guidelines and accept certain Western notions, such as the importance of couples spending time getting to know each other before marriage, we will have embarked on a slippery slope downhill. None of us can claim to be ignorant of Western society in which standards of morality and decency have plummeted to such dreadful depths that decent people are too ashamed to even discuss them. Adultery, incest, prostitution and indecency are openly and proudly flaunted in the morally-depraved hunt for new sexual thrills.

These modern realities explain the Islamic *raison d'être* for its strict codes on the Hijab, that men and women should lower their gazes in public, and that any conversations between non-Maḥrams should be formal and business-like. It is only by maintaining such high standards of conduct that the Muslim can hope to escape the depravity of family and social life found in the modern world.

THE ENGAGEMENT

When considering a proposal for marriage, both parties have been advised strongly by the Prophet ﷺ to give priority to piety and good character. However, other considerations such as appearance, financial situation, education, manners, reputation and family background are all important and should not be ignored. General compatibility is vital for any marriage to be successful. A couple who have nothing in common and find it difficult to hold a conversation together (especially if they speak different languages!) will probably not stay together for very long.

A divorcee named Fāṭimah bint Qays once came to the Prophet ﷺ and asked for his advice concerning marriage proposals she had received from the companions Muʿāwiyah and Abū Jaḥm. The Prophet ﷺ said,

> *Muʿāwiyah is a poor man, and Abu Jaḥm's shoulder is never separated from his stick (i.e, he is either violent or travels frequently). I advise you to marry ʿUsāmah bin Zayd.* (Muslim)

Fāṭimah acted upon this advice and her marriage was a happy one.

An Islamic engagement (Khuṭbah) is not considered to be a binding covenant but a promise, and it is the duty of every Muslim to abide by his promises to the best of his ability. Situations do change however, and an end to an engagement may become necessary. In such cases both parties should return any gifts they may have exchanged, and end the affair with as few recriminations as is possible.

SEEKING THE AID OF THE ALMIGHTY

Before deciding whether to accept or reject a marriage proposal, the individual must always consult his or her well-wishers, such as parents and elders. The marriage of a Muslim woman is completely invalid if she does not have the consent of her Walī (male guardian, such as her father or brother). A Muslim man has no such requirement to fulfil but the advice and consent of his family is obviously important.

The most important advice and help any of us can seek in any situation is that from Allah. The Companions reported that the Prophet ﷺ would teach them the *Du'ā Istikhārah* (seeking goodness) with as much care and regularity as he taught them Sūrah Al-Fātiḥah. It is narrated that he said, *"None fails who consults (the creatures), and none regrets who seeks goodness (from the Creator)."* (Ṭabarānī with a weak Isnād)

A problem which often confronts young men as they contemplate matrimony is whether to marry young when financially dependent on others, or to delay marriage until an income is secured. The answer to this concern comes from the Prophet ﷺ himself

> *O young men! He amongst you who is able to marry should marry, and whoever is not able should fast regularly, as this will be a shield for him.* (Bukhārī & Muslim)

INTER-FAITH MARRIAGES

A contentious issue which has confronted Muslim men is that of marriage with women of the Ahl al-Kitab (People of the Book, such as Jews and Christians). Because Islam has permitted Muslim men from entering such marriages, huge numbers of men who have emigrated to Western countries have married women who are nominally Christians. In other words, they are women for whom Christianity is often little more than celebrating Christmas once a year and ultimately being buried in a church graveyard. For the vast majority of couples these marriages have brought little happiness, especially when children have been involved. A man may be quite happy to live with a wife who drinks alcohol, dresses indecently and has no respect for his faith, but when he sees his young children being encouraged to do the same and to hate the culture and religion of their father, feelings of regret and shame often surface.

The problem has arisen because Muslims have failed to realise that the permission to marry Ahl al-Kitab women is strongly conditional. Allah Almighty says in the Qur'an,

$$ ٱلۡيَوۡمَ أُحِلَّ لَكُمُ ٱلطَّيِّبَـٰتُ وَطَعَامُ ٱلَّذِينَ أُوتُواْ ٱلۡكِتَـٰبَ حِلٌّ لَّكُمۡ وَطَعَامُكُمۡ حِلٌّ لَّهُمۡ وَٱلۡمُحۡصَنَـٰتُ مِنَ ٱلۡمُؤۡمِنَـٰتِ وَٱلۡمُحۡصَنَـٰتُ مِنَ ٱلَّذِينَ أُوتُواْ ٱلۡكِتَـٰبَ مِن قَبۡلِكُمۡ $$

Made lawful to you on this day are ... in marriage, chaste women from the believers and chaste women from those who were given the Scripture before you ... (*Sūrah al-Mā'idah*, 5:5)

Thus a Muslim man may also marry a Jewish or Christian woman who is chaste and not known for fornication. But, many Muslim men who marry outside their faith do not choose their brides for their high levels of morality, chastity or piety. Scholars have also advised that such inter-faith marriages must be practised only in Muslim lands.

Sayyidinā 'Umar, the second Caliph, used to discourage his Muslim subjects from marrying women of the Ahl Al-Kitāb. He once wrote to Hudhaifah bin Al-Yamān and advised him to divorce his Jewish wife. One of the reasons behind this action was that *Sayyidinā*

'Umar believed that by marrying Kitābī women, Muslim men would be abandoning Muslim women.

CHAPTER THREE

<u>ROLE OF THE GUARDIAN IN MARRIAGE</u>

The agreement of the bride's guardian (Walī) is an essential component of the Islamic marriage contract. The Prophet ﷺ has said, *"Any woman's marriage without the consent of her guardian is void"* (Aḥmad). The bride's guardian must be a Muslim male adult, such as her father, grandfather, uncle, brother, or even son if she is re-marrying. If she has no such guardian, the Muslim ruler of the land can take his place. In a non-Muslim country this role can be fulfilled by someone in authority such as an Imam or head of an Islamic organisation. It is often found these days that the youth and their parents have very differing views on suitable candidates for marriage. Many young Muslim women wish to be married to pious men, but their parents reject their choice on grounds not recognised by the Sharia, such as colour, racial or language prejudice. The parents may also try to force their own choice on their daughters, despite the obvious incompatibility between the couple. Muslim women in such a situation should remember that they have the full right to reject any suitors their guardians may bring forward, but this must be for genuine faults and not simply to spite their parents. This right is illustrated clearly by the following incident:

A young woman called Khansah bint Khizām once came to the Prophet ﷺ complaining that her father wished to force her to marry her cousin. The Prophet ﷺ told her that she had the right to reject her father's choice, but Khansah replied, "I accept my father's choice. But

I wished to let the people know that our guardians cannot force us in marriage." (Aḥmad, Ibn Mājah & Nasā'ī)

Those young women, who are approached by compatible suitors but find that their guardians are refusing to give their consent, often react by rebelling and making hasty decisions. It is quite common for such young ladies to run away from home to marry, appointing guardians of their own choice in order to fulfil this requirement of the marriage contract. These actions are to be deplored just as much as the prejudices and thoughtlessness of their parents.

THE MARRIAGE CEREMONY (NIKĀḤ)

The Islamic marriage ceremony is a simple affair which requires that the following four conditions must be met:

1) Consent to the marriage by both bride and groom.
2) Consent to the marriage by the guardian of the bride.
3) The presence of two witnesses.
4) An agreement on the amount of Mahr (the dower given as a gift from the groom to his bride).

The Sunnah recommends that the marriage ceremony should be preceded by a sermon (Khuṭbah). The Prophet ﷺ used to begin his marriage sermons by reciting a number of Quranic verses:

يَـٰٓأَيُّهَا ٱلنَّاسُ ٱتَّقُواْ رَبَّكُمُ ٱلَّذِى خَلَقَكُم مِّن نَّفْسٍ وَٰحِدَةٍ وَخَلَقَ مِنْهَا زَوْجَهَا وَبَثَّ مِنْهُمَا رِجَالًا كَثِيرًا وَنِسَآءً وَٱتَّقُواْ ٱللَّهَ ٱلَّذِى تَسَآءَلُونَ بِهِۦ وَٱلْأَرْحَامَ إِنَّ ٱللَّهَ كَانَ عَلَيْكُمْ رَقِيبًا

O Mankind ! Be dutiful to your Lord. Who created you from a single man, and from him He created his wife, and from them both He created many men and women. And fear Allah through Whom you demand your mutual rights, and do your duty to the relations of the

wombs. Surely Allah is a Watcher over you! (*Sūrah An-Nisā'*, 4:1)

يَـٰٓأَيُّهَا ٱلَّذِينَ ءَامَنُواْ ٱتَّقُواْ ٱللَّهَ حَقَّ تُقَاتِهِۦ وَلَا تَمُوتُنَّ إِلَّا وَأَنتُم مُّسۡلِمُونَ

O you who believe! Fear Allah as He should be feared, and die not except in total submission to Allah. (*Sūrah Āl 'Imrān*, 3:102)

يَـٰٓأَيُّهَا ٱلَّذِينَ ءَامَنُواْ ٱتَّقُواْ ٱللَّهَ وَقُولُواْ قَوۡلًا سَدِيدًا ۝ يُصۡلِحۡ لَكُمۡ أَعۡمَـٰلَكُمۡ وَيَغۡفِرۡ لَكُمۡ ذُنُوبَكُمۡ وَمَن يُطِعِ ٱللَّهَ وَرَسُولَهُۥ فَقَدۡ فَازَ فَوۡزًا عَظِيمًا

O you who believe! Fear Allah, and always speak the truth. He will direct you to righteous deeds, and will Forgive you your sins. Whoever obeys Allah and His Messenger has indeed achieved a great success. (*Sūrah Al-Aḥzāb*, 33:70-71)

The Prophet would then stress the importance of marriage by saying: *Marriage is from my Sunnah. Marry women who are beloved and loving and bear children, because I shall be proud of my Ummah on the Day Judgment.* (Abū Dāwūd & Nasā'ī)

The marriage is usually conducted by a Qāḍī or an Imam, and once his marriage sermon is over, he will ask the bride's guardian to say to the groom, "I wed to you so-and-so, of whom I am a guardian. The amount of dower is such-and-such, to be paid either now or later." The groom will accept this proposal and the couple will now be married. The consent of the bride is usually obtained before this Nikāḥ ceremony.

One should notice that all three of the above Quranic verses emphasise the importance of Taqwā (piety and fear of Allah). This is because human legislation and punishments can never hope to change bad characters and prevent the evils which destroy so many marriages. Laws, the police and jail sentences are no solution to cruelty, disobedience, lying, desertion and infidelity. The only real deterrent to all such vices and evils is fear of Allah and an awareness of the retribution awaiting mankind on the Day of Judgment. Within the four walls of his home, the only thing which can stop a man from bullying, abusing and even beating his wife is the fear of The Omnipresent, Allah. A couple who do not have this fear of Allah will spend their lives at the mercy of temptations and desires, and betraying each other will become very easy.

DOWRY AND DOWER

The Mahr (dower) should not be confused with the Dowry. The Dowry is an ancient and common practice found in most Asian, African and Middle Eastern societies, and refers to the huge numbers of gifts given by the bride's family to the groom and his family at the time of marriage. These gifts often reach exorbitant sums well outside the reach of ordinary people, and it is not uncommon for the groom's family to send long lists of gifts required once the couple are betrothed, threatening a quick divorce or even death if their requirements are not met. A daughter's marriage can become a huge burden for poor parents, and this is partly why the birth of a girl is with gloom and despondency in many Eastern societies.

Needless to say, Islam takes a dim view of such practices and beliefs. The only Dowry to be found in Islamic practice is the obvious natural one of parents giving gifts to their own daughter at the time of her marriage. The Prophet ﷺ gave his daughter Fāṭimah, at the time of her marriage to ʿAlī, household objects such as a dress, a jug and a pillow stuffed with grass.

The Islamic Mahr (dower) is a gift given by the husband to his new wife at the time of marriage. It should be fixed according to the financial status of the couple and is recorded in the marriage contract. The Prophet used to recommend small dowers, saying, *"The less the expenses involved in a marriage, the more blessed it will be"* (A similar text is narrated by Imam Aḥmad). The word "expenses" in this Ḥadīth refers to the dower, which can be cash, jewellery or other valuable items. But as the following incident shows, a service that the husband provides for his wife (in this case, teaching her Sūrahs of the Quran) can also be her dower:

A woman came to the Prophet ﷺ and said, "O Messenger of Allah! I have dedicated (Cf. *Sūrah Al-Aḥzāb,*33:50) myself to you." She then stood therefore a long time, so a man got up and said, "O Messenger of Allah! Marry me to her if you have no need of her." The Messenger of Allah ﷺ asked, *"Do you have anything you can give her as dower?"* He replied, "I have nothing except this waistcloth of mine." The Prophet ﷺ said, *"If you gave her your waistcloth, you would be left without one, so find something else."* The man said. "I do not have anything" to which the Prophet ﷺ said, *"Find something, even if it is only an iron ring."* So he sought but found nothing, so the Prophet asked, *"Do you have (in your heart) any of the Quran?"* The man replied, "Yes, Sūrahs such-and-such," naming them, so the Prophet ﷺ said to him, *"I marry you to her with the dower of what you have memorised of the Quran"* (Bukhārī & Muslim).

The modern trend of agreeing on colossal sums of dower in order to impress the people, despite the fact that the bridegroom will have great difficulty in acquiring that sum, are merely a sign of people's obsession with wealth and ostentation, and so should not be encouraged. The dower given by the Prophet ﷺ to his first wife Khadījah was 12 and a half Uqiyyah of gold, equivalent to 500 Dirhams. But the dower he gave to his other wives and fixed for his own daughters never exceeded 400 Dirhams. The only exception was Umm Ḥabībah who was in Ethiopia at the time of her marriage, and the King Negus of Ethiopia gave her a large Mahr on behalf of the Prophet ﷺ.

The marriage contract remains valid in situations where the Mahr was not fixed at the time of marriage. In such cases the dower is still payable but will be decided in accordance with the status of the woman by looking at the dowers of other women in her family.

When the marriage ceremony has been concluded, guests are encouraged to congratulate the couple by saying, *"May Allah bless you both, and may your union be happy"* (Abū Dāwūd & Tirmidhī). It is an Islamic requirement that the bridegroom should invite guests to a marriage feast, called the Walīmah, after consummation. It is a common Muslim practice for the family of the bride to also invite guests to a wedding feast on the day of the Nikāḥ. Marriage is a happy occasion for all parties concerned and must be made public. The Prophet ﷺ has said, *"Announce marriages publicly, hold them inside the Mosques, and beat the daff (drum) on these occasions"* (Abū Dāwūd, the part *"hold them in the mosques"* is regarded as weak by Shaikh Al-Albānī).

CHAPTER FOUR

<u>PRAYING FOR A RIGHTEOUS CHILD</u>

The life of a Muslim is governed by the remembrance of Allah at each and every opportunity. This is true even when a man approaches his wife for sexual fulfilment, as he has been told to offer the following supplication first: *"O Allah! Keep us away from Satan, and keep Satan away from whatever You bestow upon us"* (Bukhārī, Muslim, Abū Dāwūd & Tirmidhī).

In his daily prayers he should always remember to ask Allah for pious offspring. The Quran has recorded this supplication for all believers and slaves of Allah:

$$وَٱلَّذِينَ يَقُولُونَ رَبَّنَا هَبْ لَنَا مِنْ أَزْوَاجِنَا وَذُرِّيَّتِنَا قُرَّةَ أَعْيُنٍ وَٱجْعَلْنَا لِلْمُتَّقِينَ إِمَامًا$$

Our Lord! Bestow on us wives and offspring who will be the comfort of our eyes, and make us leaders of the pious people. (*Sūrah al-Furqān, 25:74*)

On the Day of Judgment each individual will stand trembling in fear in front of Allah, and standing behind him will be his progeny. His prayers and efforts in life should therefore be that he will be the Imam and ancestor of pious Muslims, not of murderers and criminals.

The birth of a child should always be an occasion for joy and celebration. The Prophets of Allah were often given the good news of children even before they were born. In Sūrah Āl ‘Imrān, the Quran tells the story of Prophet Zakariyyah ﷺ who was extremely surprised to see Maryam, peace be upon her, receiving fruits which were out of season and therefore impossible to obtain. When he asked her where the fruit had come from, she replied that,

هُوَ مِنْ عِندِ ٱللَّهِ إِنَّ ٱللَّهَ يَرْزُقُ مَن يَشَآءُ بِغَيْرِ حِسَابٍ

They are from Allah, for Allah provides to whom He wishes without counting. (*Sūrah Āl ‘Imrān*, 3:37)

Prophet Zakariyyah and his wife were childless and as both had reached old-age, they had given up hope of having children. He now realised that if Allah could provide Maryam with fruits which were out of season, He could just as easily give a child to an old couple. He thus prayed to Allah for a pious child:

هُنَالِكَ دَعَا زَكَرِيَّا رَبَّهُ قَالَ رَبِّ هَبْ لِي مِن لَّدُنكَ ذُرِّيَّةً طَيِّبَةً إِنَّكَ سَمِيعُ ٱلدُّعَآءِ ۞ فَنَادَتْهُ ٱلْمَلَٰٓئِكَةُ وَهُوَ قَآئِمٌ يُصَلِّي فِي ٱلْمِحْرَابِ أَنَّ ٱللَّهَ يُبَشِّرُكَ بِيَحْيَىٰ مُصَدِّقًا بِكَلِمَةٍ مِّنَ ٱللَّهِ وَسَيِّدًا وَحَصُورًا وَنَبِيًّا مِّنَ ٱلصَّٰلِحِينَ

"O my Lord! Grant me from You a good offspring. You are indeed the Hearer of all supplications." Then the angels called him while he was standing in prayer in the Miḥrāb, saying, "Allah gives you glad tidings of Yaḥyā, confirming the Word of Allah (i.e. Prophet ‘Isā). He will be noble, celibate, a Prophet, from among the righteous." (*Sūrah Āl ‘Imrān*, 3:38-39)

As Prophet ‘Isā ﷺ has said, if a person asks Allah for bread, Allah Almighty will not give him stones. A pious person who prays to his Lord for good things will not have his prayers rejected. Prophet Zakariyyah prayed for a pious child, and the angels gave him the good news of a noble and chaste son who would also be a Prophet.

Prophet Ibrāhīm was also old and childless as his wife Ḥajrah was barren. He too was given the good news of two sons, Ismāʿīl and Isḥāq, and of a grandson Yaʿqūb, all of whom would be Prophets. Ibrāhīm had prayed to Allah,

$$ رَبِّ هَبْ لِي مِنَ ٱلصَّٰلِحِينَ ۝ فَبَشَّرْنَٰهُ بِغُلَٰمٍ حَلِيمٍ $$

"My Lord! Grant me offspring from the righteous." So We gave him the glad tidings of a patient son (Ismāʿīl). (*Sūrah aṣ-Ṣāffāt*, 37:100-101)

About Sārah, the second wife of Ibrāhīm, the Quran speaks as follows:

$$ وَٱمْرَأَتُهُۥ قَآئِمَةٌ فَضَحِكَتْ فَبَشَّرْنَٰهَا بِإِسْحَٰقَ وَمِن وَرَآءِ إِسْحَٰقَ يَعْقُوبَ ۝ قَالَتْ يَٰوَيْلَتَىٰٓ ءَأَلِدُ وَأَنَا۠ عَجُوزٌ وَهَٰذَا بَعْلِي شَيْخًا ۖ إِنَّ هَٰذَا لَشَىْءٌ عَجِيبٌ ۝ قَالُوٓا۟ أَتَعْجَبِينَ مِنْ أَمْرِ ٱللَّهِ ۖ رَحْمَتُ ٱللَّهِ وَبَرَكَٰتُهُۥ عَلَيْكُمْ أَهْلَ ٱلْبَيْتِ ۚ إِنَّهُۥ حَمِيدٌ مَّجِيدٌ $$

We gave her glad tidings of Isḥāq, and after Isḥāq, of Yaʿqūb. She said in astonishment, "Woe unto me! Shall I bear a child while I am an old woman, and here is my husband, an old man? Indeed this is a strange thing." The angels said, "Do you wonder at the Decree of Allah? The Mercy of Allah and His Blessings be upon you, O family of Ibrāhīm! Surely Allah is Praiseworthy, Glorious!" (*Sūrah Hūd*, 11:71-73)

Maryam was also conveyed the good news of a son by the angels:

$$ إِذْ قَالَتِ ٱلْمَلَٰٓئِكَةُ يَٰمَرْيَمُ إِنَّ ٱللَّهَ يُبَشِّرُكِ بِكَلِمَةٍ مِّنْهُ ٱسْمُهُ ٱلْمَسِيحُ عِيسَى ٱبْنُ مَرْيَمَ وَجِيهًا فِي ٱلدُّنْيَا وَٱلْءَاخِرَةِ وَمِنَ ٱلْمُقَرَّبِينَ $$

Remember when the angels said, "O Maryam! Indeed Allah gives you the glad tidings of a Word from Him. His name will be the Messiah 'Isā, the son of Maryam, held in honour in this world and in the hereafter, and of those brought near to Allah." (*Sūrah Āl 'Imrān*, 3:45)

THE BIRTH OF A CHILD

Parents are often quick to criticise their offspring for not treating them with the respect and love due to parents, but they forget that children too have rights, even before they are born. One of the most important of these rights is that the child should be legitimate. An adulterous couple deny this right to their child for its entire life, and this is one of the reasons why the Islamic punishment for adultery is so severe. Secondly, both parents contribute not only to the genetic and physical characteristics of their child, but also to his mental and moral health. An adulterous couple at the time of intimacy know that they are cheating and being immoral, almost like thieves. These feelings of guilt and wrong doing will be passed through to the child conceived from that union. Their child will grow up to be aware that he was illegitimate, even if his parents married later, and the detrimental effect of this on his own moral standards cannot be ignored.

The months between conception and birth require extreme care on the part of the mother. Her baby will be affected by everything: the food she eats, the drinks she takes, the physical exercise she gets, her mental thoughts and emotions, and even her spiritual devotions. Everything she does is transmitted to her child, and so she alone is responsible for the well-being of her offspring from conception to birth. For example, women who smoke heavily in pregnancy are at increased risk of having premature babies.

But the real task begins when the child finally enters this world. From then on, the welfare of their child will dominate the thoughts and actions of the parents. But first, a brief look at some of the immediate steps which should be taken after the birth of a child:

The Adhān

The first name to pass through the new-born's ear should be the name of Allah. For this purpose the Prophet ﷺ taught us to pronounce the Adhān in a very low voice in the child's right ear.

It should be noted that no prayer is held after the Adhān is given in the ear of a new born child. The opposite is however true when a person dies, as a funeral prayer is held but no Adhān is given before it. It seems that a call for prayer is said whenever a child is born, but the prayer is held when that individual dies. Life is thus the short time-span between an Adhān and the prayer. It is a precious time which can never return, and so none of it should be wasted. In our daily lives when we hear the call for prayer, many of us abandon our worldly pursuits and use the short gap between the Adhān and its prayer to prepare for that prayer. We perform the ablution and hurry to the mosques, preparing ourselves physically and mentally for communion with our Creator. Similarly, the goal of life should be to prepare for that final funeral prayer.

Taḥnīk

The Prophet ﷺ used to practice Taḥnīk, which was to chew a small piece of date in his mouth until soft, and then gently rub some of it on the upper palate of the infant's mouth. If dates are not available, a sweet substitute such as honey may be used.

Removing the Hair

It is a Sunnah to shave the baby's head completely on the seventh day after birth. The equivalent weight in silver of this hair is then given in charity to the poor. The hairs which grew inside the womb are considered to be impure and so are completely removed. The Prophet ﷺ used to draw comparisons between the sinless state of such a child and a person who shaves his head after the Hajj. He said, *"He who performs the Hajj without any obscene actions or sins is just like a new-born baby"* (Muslim, Tirmidhī & others).

ʿAqīqah

The Prophet ﷺ used to perform the ʿAqīqah of each new baby on the seventh day after its birth. He used to say that each child is held under mortgage until its ʿAqīqah has been performed (Abū Dāwūd & Tirmidhī).

Thus parents who do not perform the ʿAqīqah at its correct time can do it later, although the best dates are the seventh, 14th or even 21st day after the child's birth. The practice of the Prophet ﷺ was to sacrifice two sheep at the birth of a boy and one sheep at the birth of a girl. Friends and family were then invited to the ʿAqīqah feast to celebrate the happy occasion.

Sadly, for an increasing number of parents living in the West today, the fact that it is not easy to buy live sheep and then slaughter them in their back-gardens has become an excuse for apathy and disregard of this important Sunnah. The same is unfortunately also true of ʿEid Al-Aḍḥā, the Festival of Sacrifice celebrated on 10 Dhu 'l-Ḥijjah, when each Muslim household is required to make a sacrificial offering. This festival as well as the ʿAqīqah often pass by without the required celebration because the sacrifice is considered to be too much of a burden. For many Muslims an easy solution has been to send money abroad, either to relatives "back home" or to Muslim aid agencies, who promise to offer the sacrifice on their behalf. Indeed many Muslim organisations encourage this practice actively, suggesting that we should not be consuming the sacrificial meat when there are so many millions of Muslims starving throughout the world.

Yes, the dreadful state of the Muslim Ummah is an indisputable fact, but this does not in any way legitimise the abandonment of our Prophet's ﷺ Sunnah. The sin of abandoning a Sunnah is severe, and many young Muslims are growing up in the West never having seen a sheep being slaughtered for 'Eid or for an 'Aqīqah. Their only memories concerning these two sacrifices is that of sending a cheque abroad! For the next generations of Muslims being born and raised in the west, 'Eid Al-Aḍḥā, and the 'Aqīqah will become so synonymous with sending charity abroad that they may never even realise that the cheque has replaced a sacrifice.

Muslims should always remember the plight of their less fortunate brothers and sisters throughout the world, especially at times of joy and celebrations. Charity should be given regularly to help the needy and to cleanse our souls from love of material things, but charity cannot replace a Sunnah practiced without fail by our beloved Prophet ﷺ.

Sending money abroad also deprives families of the sense of occasion and celebration that 'Eid and 'Aqīqah have to offer. The activities of travelling to an abattoir, choosing and slaughtering a sheep, cooking it and sharing it with friends and relatives will automatically become a time for people to get together and enjoy the celebration. Older children will especially remember the birth of their younger siblings by their 'Aqīqah celebrations, and this sense of occasion can never be achieved by sending money abroad.

Circumcision

Circumcision of male children is a compulsory Islamic requirement. It is recommended to perform it in the early days of infancy as this is easier and the wound heals more swiftly than if it is performed later.

Naming the Child

It is the duty of the parents to choose their child's name wisely, as he or she will carry it for the rest of their lives. The Prophet ﷺ

recommended names which contain Allah's attributes and reflect the person's servitude to Allah, such as 'Abdullāh (slave of Allah) and 'Abdur-Raḥmān (slave of the Merciful), the female equivalents of which would be Amatullāh and Amatur-Raḥman. Other names with pleasant meanings, such as the names of Prophets and Companions are also recommended. Names which have non-Islamic connotations or are associated with un-Islamic beliefs must not be kept by Muslims.

In the Arab tradition, a Kunyah or by-name, beginning with "Abū (father of)" or "Umm (mother of)" can also be added. Parents often take the names of their first-born children for their Kunyah, so for example, the parents of a boy called Muḥammad would call themselves Abū Muḥammad and Umm Muḥammad. Our Prophet ﷺ was known as Abū l-Qāsim, after his first son al-Qāsim who died in infancy. His wife 'Ā'ishah, the Mother of the Believers, had no children of her own, so she took the Kunyah Umm 'Abdillāh from her sister Asmā's son, 'Abdullāh bin al-Zubair.

Names with good meanings were considered to be so important that the Prophet ﷺ would change any names with unpleasant meanings. One of his Companions was a man named Ḥazan (rocky tract), which the Messenger changed to Sahl (easy). A woman called 'Āsiyyah (sinful) had her name changed by the Prophet ﷺ to Jamīlah (beautiful). The name of a person can have a great effect on the life of a person. *Sayyidinā* 'Umar was once sitting with a group of people when a man introduced himself as Jamarah (light coal). 'Umar asked the man his father's name, which he gave as Shihāb (blazing fire). 'Umar then asked him the name of the region he came from, to which the man replied, "Ḥurqah (burning)." 'Umar asked him for the name of his street, to which the reply he received was Dhāt-Laza (blazing fire). *Sayyidinā* 'Umar then ordered the man to hurry home as he suspected that his house may have been on fire. The man rushed home, and found that his house really was on fire! (*Muwaṭṭā'* of Imam Mālik)

RIGHTS OF THE CHILD

Children have rights over their parents from a young age, including suckling, maintenance and education. The following incident which took place during the time of *Sayyidinā* 'Umar illustrates this point:

A man once came to the Second Caliph with his young son, complaining that the boy was disobedient and insolent to his parents. Instead of admonishing the boy, 'Umar calmly asked him why he did not obey his parents. The boy replied by asking, "Do I not have rights over my father? Are there not certain things which he should do for me?" 'Umar replied that the child naturally has rights over his parents, and when the boy asked to hear some of these, he said,

> When a man wishes to marry, he should marry a pious woman to be the mother of his children. When Allah Almighty blesses him with a child he should give him a pleasant name. He should teach the child Quran and Ḥadīth. When the child reaches the age of majority, he should arrange for his or her marriage.

The boy was listening quietly and now said,

> My father did none of these for me. As far as my mother is concerned, my father married a woman who belonged to a certain group of immoral people. I do not wish to name these people, but they are known for their illegal sexual relations. When I was born my father named me Khunfasa (black beetle). Wherever I go, I am taunted by other children of being a cockroach. My father did not arrange for my Islamic education. I have never attended a Mosque or Madrasah, and I have no knowledge of Quran or Ḥadīth.

When the boy had finished his complaint 'Umar turned to the father and said, "You have severed relations with your son before he severed relations with you." (*Tarbiyyah Al-Awlād*, 'Abdullāh Nāṣir 'Ulwān)

SUCKLING

The Quran gives the following advice to mothers:

وَٱلْوَٰلِدَٰتُ يُرْضِعْنَ أَوْلَٰدَهُنَّ حَوْلَيْنِ كَامِلَيْنِ

The mothers are to suckle their infants for two years.
(*Sūrah al-Baqarah*, 2:233)

The early formative years in a child's life are crucial for his emotional and physical health during the rest of his life. Health experts agree that breast-feeding is the best way to feed a baby as it is designed to meet all of the baby's nutritional needs. The mother's milk is easily digested, contains antibodies and anti-allergens. Studies have shown that such babies are healthier than bottle-fed babies and have fewer respiratory, gastrointestinal and middle-ear infections.

It is the duty of the husband to work hard and provide for his family, so that his wife can have the freedom to stay at home and provide a decent and pure Islamic life style for their children. It is only such mothers who can suckle their children for the full two years with ease. Ironically, many women think it is respectable to labour for other people, whether teaching them, treating them or cleaning up after them, but degrading to work equally hard for their own families.

MAINTENANCE

Providing for all the legitimate needs of his family is the main duty of the father. He should ensure that his family have food, clothes, medical attention, a roof over their heads and all their other daily needs. The Prophet ﷺ once said, *"The sin of not providing maintenance is enough to waste the person's deeds."* (Aḥmad & Abū Dāwūd)

It should be remembered that the income a father brings home should be from Halal sources, as living off Haram earnings brings down Allah's Wrath on the family and ensures that their prayers to Him are rejected.

CHAPTER FIVE

<u>THE VALUE OF ISLAMIC EDUCATION</u>

The predominant youth culture we see around us is one of rebellion, suspicion of authority, individualism and immorality. The lack of discipline and strong moral codes has resulted in an obsession with drugs, all-night rave parties, sexual experimenting, gender confusion and violence. The frightening aspect is that this scenario is not the sole preserve of any culture or country but of the entire world. Cinema, internet and satellite television have thrust decadence and immorality into all homes and societies and it would be very naive of Muslim parents to believe that they can protect and shield their children from the evils around them completely. This could only be achieved by destroying their television sets, newspapers and books, and forbidding their children from attending non-Muslim schools or universities. Such drastic measures would be extremist, impractical and may even backfire. Muslim parents must therefore accept that their children will eventually have to mix in society and will quickly become aware of the good and especially of the evil that exists around them. The sensible solution is thus to give children a thorough and solid Islamic education from a very early age, and to instil in them a deep sense of Islamic values and morals, so that they will be able to separate the good from the evil for themselves. Parents cannot always be on hand to advise their children, but their teachings and guidance will remain with their children wherever they may go and whichever situation may confront them.

The state of our Muslim youth everywhere shows clearly how lacking many parents are in the field of Islamic education. Fathers are especially guilty as they often believe that their only duty is to provide financially for their families, and once they have done so they are happy to take a back-seat in the affairs of the home. Yet the Prophet ﷺ has said, "*No father can give his child a better gift than good manners, good character and a good education*" (Tirmidhī).

The story is told of a woman in the second century A.H. who had arranged for her young son to be apprenticed to a baker. The child was very young, but the mother was poor and needed his wages. Some time later she went to visit her son and found him absent from the baker's shop. On inquiring, she was told that he had been taken to the Mosque, so she followed and found her son being taught in the front row of the Mosque. Furiously, she demanded that her son be allowed to return to work as she needed his income. The teacher offered instead to pay her the child's wages himself in return for the child becoming a full-time student in the Mosque, an offer which the mother accepted.

This teacher was none other than Imam Abū Ḥanīfah, one of the four great Imams, and the little boy was Imam Abū Yūsuf, who became one of Imam Abū Ḥanīfah's greatest students and the Supreme Judge in the Court of the 'Abbasid Caliph Hārūn al-Rashīd.

EDUCATION IN EARLY CHILDHOOD

The first stage in a child's education is the period between birth and Tamyīz (age of distinction), which is approximately five years. At this stage the child is like a dry sponge, ready to absorb any moisture it comes across. Too many parents treat their infants as unintelligent creatures who play, eat and sleep, forgetting that these are the most formative years in the child's life.

Beginning with nutrition, the child should be suckled by his own mother for the first two years of his life, instead of being given powdered milk which has been stored in tins for months. Few adults would abandon fresh fruit and vegetables for stale, tinned foods, yet they are quite happy to feed nothing but tinned milk and foods to their infants. Secondly, just as the mother's blood in the womb passes nutrients and her emotions through to the blood of her child, so her milk also passes her characteristics and emotions to her child. A happy and relaxed mother will convey these feelings of tranquillity to her child while she is suckling him, causing him to feel immense comfort and confidence.

A child is born with reflexes, instincts and natural capacity, and his parents can train him in Islam through all these three categories. For example, the reflexes all children have include coughing, sneezing and yawning. The mother plays a unique position in this training as she is with the child all day and night, and so she can mould the child's response to these reflexes in an Islamic manner. So each time the child sneezes, she can say slowly and aloud "Al-Ḥamdu lillāh". The child will become so accustomed to hearing this Du'ā each time he hears a sneeze that the two will form an automatic association in his mind.

MOULDING NATURAL INSTINCTS

The value of good training is such that it can transform the natural instincts of a creature beyond recognition- For example, the natural instinct of a dog when it comes across a weak or dead animal is to fight and tear at the flesh violently. Yet the Quran mentions how even such a dangerous beast can help man acquire Halal food:

$$قُلْ أُحِلَّ لَكُمُ ٱلطَّيِّبَٰتُ وَمَا عَلَّمْتُم مِّنَ ٱلْجَوَارِحِ مُكَلِّبِينَ تُعَلِّمُونَهُنَّ مِمَّا عَلَّمَكُمُ ٱللَّهُ فَكُلُوا۟ مِمَّآ أَمْسَكْنَ عَلَيْكُمْ وَٱذْكُرُوا۟ ٱسْمَ ٱللَّهِ عَلَيْهِ$$

Say: "Lawful for you are ... those beasts and birds of prey which you have trained like dogs, teaching them to hunt game in the manner directed to you by Allah. So eat what they catch for you, but pronounce the Name of Allah over it." (*Sūrah al-Mā'idah*, 5:4)

The explanation of this verse is that an untrained dog which catches an animal shot by a hunter will instinctively bite and tear at the animal, thus making the food Haram. But a trained dog is far superior and will bring the catch back to his master without biting it, even though he may be hungry. Such food is Halal for consumption.

If the value of good and early training is such that it can discipline a dog against its natural instincts, imagine what it can do for a young and innocent child. As an example, all children pass water instinctively whenever the need arises, and parents have to train their children at some stage to do so not in their clothes but in the toilet. Muslim parents need to go a step further, teaching the child not to urinate standing, to wash himself always with his left hand, and to ensure that dirty water does not splash back on his own body.

The practice of encouraging the development of sexual instincts from a young age is to be deplored, and the harmful effects of it are quite plain to see. Children are naturally curious and introducing them to a subject such as sex or child-birth, albeit in simple terms, is sure to arouse their curiosity even further. For example, telling a child that the bulge in his mother's midriff contains a new baby is a common practice in today's society. Indeed midwives and nurses actively encourage parents to prepare children for a new sibling. It is only inevitable that the small child will then ask how the baby got into the mother, and how it will come out.

Childhood is a time of innocence and parents should aim to keep their children innocent for as long as possible.

KINDERGARTENS

Private kindergartens will admit children full-time from birth, to allow mothers the convenience of leaving their new-borns with strangers every day while they themselves go to work. It is no wonder that such children grow up to feel little emotional attachment for their parents, and when the roles are reversed and the parents become old and incapable of taking care of themselves, their children feel no qualms about abandoning them to the care of strangers in old people's homes.

In Britain, school education becomes compulsory for all children from the age of five years, but to send them for long hours to kindergartens or nurseries before this age is not recommended. A kindergarten who spends most of his days in a non-Muslim environment will fail to develop a strong Islamic identity early in his life, and so his parents will have to struggle to remedy this later. The child who has been singing nursery rhymes and playing with musical instruments all day at the nursery will not only be too tired when he gets home to learn anything from his parents, but he will also find sitting down to learn the Quranic alphabet a tedious chore. The obvious exception to this would be a nursery organised by Muslim parents where the children would be taught in an Islamic manner.

Conversely, a child who spends the early formative years of his life with his family in an Islamic environment will grow up to be a Muslim first and foremost. His manners, instincts, interests, hobbies, behaviour and thoughts will have been disciplined and trained according to the teachings of his family and not those of western teachers. For example, children enjoy imitating others, and a small child will observe his mother regularly stopping her work to perform Wuḍū' and pray. At first he will not understand why she is ignoring him, so he will attempt to distract her. By the time he is two years old, he will have accepted that prayer is a special time when no amount of tears or silly antics will win his mother's attention, so he will begin to imitate her instead, especially when he sees that this wins his mother's approval. If his mother is in the habit of praying or reciting the Quran aloud, the toddler will quickly begin to learn words and phrases automatically.

By the time the child is five years old, he will know many Du'ās, all the actions of prayer, and will have started to read the Quran. His identity, personality and habits will be strongly Islamic if the environment in his home is Islamic. For example, when he sneezes he will instinctively say, "Alhamdulillah" even if his teacher tells him to say, "Excuse me."

CHAPTER SIX

<u>FROM FIVE YEARS TO PUBERTY, INTRODUCE THEM TO ALLAH</u>

In this school-phase the imagination of the child is at its most vivid. Whatever he reads or hears about will immediately take concrete shape in his mind. Some parents make the mistake of forcing their children's obedience by using threats of ghosts, jinn, black dogs and fearsome old men. This is not advisable as it can lead to nightmares and turn the children into cowards. Discipline is vitally important at this stage, but it must be achieved wisely and can be used to direct the child towards love and fear of Allah. When the child does something wrong, he should be reprimanded gently, told why his action was wrong, and told that not only did it displease his parents, but also Allah Almighty. Ask the child if he could bear to place his finger in a small flame, and then tell him about the fires of hell which burn 70 times more fiercely. More importantly, when the child is good the parents should show their pleasure and approval, and remind him that Allah is also pleased and has prepared Paradise for such good people.

This phase is also the period of prayer. The Prophet ﷺ has commanded us,

> *Command your children to pray at the age of seven. At the age of ten, punish them if they do not pray often, and separate their beds.* (Abū Dāwūd & Ḥākim)

The wisdom behind this commandment is quite evident. Although prayer does not become obligatory until puberty, it requires firm discipline and learning which must be achieved much earlier. If not, the individual will be told to pray regularly when he reaches puberty, and will find its sudden and rigorous discipline difficult to maintain. Learning a large number of Du'ās and Quranic Sūrahs in a short space of time will also be difficult. It is part of the nature of man to become accustomed to things to which he has had constant exposure. This explains the creed behind television and road-side advertising, because constant reminders of a product make the viewer accept them subconsciously. A child who has been taught to pray regularly from the age of seven will accept prayer as part of his normal daily habit. If however after three years of such rigorous training the child shows no inclination to pray, parents must then turn their attentions towards punishment. Prayer should not be taught as an empty and meaningless ritual which can be accomplished at speed, but as a time of dialogue between the person and his Creator, a time of reflection, gratitude and forgiveness from sins. The fact that a seven-year-old should be taught to pray also implies that he should know how to perform Wuḍū' and Ṭahārah.

The order to separate the beds of brothers and sisters at the age of 10 has been given in some Hadith because sexual feelings can begin to awaken at this age. British and American news reports have recently been carrying dreadful stories of incest between family members. This is not surprising bearing in mind the total lack of modesty in homes, the open and frank discussions of sexual matters, and practices such as that of semi-nude bathing of all family members on beaches.

This is also the age to encourage good, healthy hobbies in children, such as horse-riding, swimming and target- shooting. Such outdoor activities are beneficial for children's health and help them prepare for Jihad. As Hajjāj bin Yūsuf once said, teaching children to swim is more important than teaching them to write. If they cannot write, someone else will write for them. But if they are drowning, no-one else can swim for them. And our Prophet ﷺ has said,

The strong believer is better and more beloved to Allah than the weak believer, but there is good in both. (Muslim)

The ability to memorise is strongest in childhood. Any poems, stories and Sūrahs the child learns in his early years will always remain in his memory. The child's voice can also be moulded to pronounce certain sounds. Parents should therefore realise the importance of teaching their children to recite the Quran beautifully, melodiously and correctly from a young age, and to learn a large number of Sūrahs. Children who begin to read the Quran once they have reached their teens often find it difficult, especially if Arabic is not their mother tongue. The Prophet ﷺ has advised us to recite the Quran clearly and melodiously as even the angels congregate to listen to a good recitation. Once the child has mastered the art of reciting the Quran, attention should be directed to its meaning, and simple but common words should be taught, such as Qalam (pen), Kitāb (book), Nabī (Prophet) and Ar-Raḥmān (the Merciful).

Children are inquisitive at this age and question everything around them. Parents should not ignore their thirst for knowledge but should answer them with wisdom. For example, if a child asks why the autumn leaves are turning yellow and falling to the ground, the parent can use the opportunity to talk about the cycle of life and death for all living things, and also the importance of using one's short life to do good deeds.

Parents should also set an example by speaking the truth themselves at all times and encouraging their children to do the same. Lying is one of the major signs of hypocrisy and should therefore be avoided. In a famous incident, *Sayyidinā* 'Umar and one of his Companions were travelling in the desert when they met a young shepherd boy tending his sheep. 'Umar asked the boy to slaughter a sheep for them as they were travellers and very hungry. The boy refused, citing the reason that the sheep did not belong to him but to his master. 'Umar wished to test the boy's honesty further, so he insisted, saying that as the master was not present the boy could do as he wished. The boy finished the discussion by responding that his master was not present, but Allah Almighty was watching everything. *Sayyidinā* 'Umar was so impressed by the young boy's honesty that he took him by the hand to his master and asked for the price of his freedom. The price was given and the boy was set free. *Sayyidinā* 'Umar then said to the boy, "Your statement that Allah is watching you set you free in this world, and I hope that it will also set you free in the Hereafter." (*Tarbiyyah Al-Awlād*)

Other mannerisms which children must be introduced to from a young age include Islamic greetings and table etiquettes. The Prophet ﷺ once told a child who was not eating with proper etiquettes, "*O little boy! Begin with the Name of Allah, then eat with your right hand, and eat from what is near you on the dish*" (Bukhārī & Muslim).

Children should also be accustomed to going to bed early so that they can rise for Fajr prayer without difficulty. They should also learn to begin the day not with playing but with education and learning. However, playing and general exercise are also part of young children's' learning processes and so adequate time must be made for these.

FROM CHILDHOOD TO ADULTHOOD

Teenage years are the years of hormonal and physical changes as the child develops into an adult. Sexual feelings begin to mature quickly, and for this reason parents must be careful about their child's friends, hobbies and other activities. It is necessary to keep these teenagers busy with studies, useful hobbies and Islamic activities. Good friends are obviously important for all people, as it is our friends which often determine which way we shall go, but peer pressure is at its strongest for teenagers. I used to regularly visit prisons to lead the Muslim inmates in prayer and listen to their grievances, and so I often questioned them about the events which led to their incarceration. Many prisoners I met were convicted of drug-smuggling offences, but few admit to being guilty of the crime. The excuse they often give is that friends left packages with them for safe-keeping or asked them to take a package abroad. When the police raided their homes or checked their luggage, they found drugs or stolen goods. These excuses may be true, but I often wonder what sort of a man would keep such close company with racketeers, thieves and drug-pushers. The Prophet of Allah ﷺ has told us, *"A person is upon the religion of his friends, so see whom you take as a friend."* (Tirmidhī, Abū Dāwūd & Aḥmad)

These days young boys are especially notorious for getting involved in activities of which they do not approve but nevertheless are forced to join in order to win the approval of their peers. The main reason why gangs of youth steal cars for joy riding, vandalise properties and experiment with drugs is often because they are unemployed and bored. Their bodies and minds are charged with energy but they often have no legitimate outlet for this energy and so resort to crime. Parents need to be aware of the frustrations and shattered dreams of the youth, especially in the high unemployment climate of today. Further education, apprenticeships and even low-paid work are preferable to unemployment, boredom and frustration.

Parents should also ensure that their youngsters are surrounded by good company which will lead them to mosques rather than pubs.

The youth also need people to talk to, who will listen to and understand their difficulties. The first port-of-call should ideally be that of parents, in the knowledge that they have a close and warm relationship with their parents. This kind of rapport between parents and children cannot be created overnight but is a long process which begins when the child is young. Unfortunately many Muslim youth feel alienated from their parents, especially their fathers. They inevitably turn to people outside the home for guidance and comfort, often untrustworthy friends and non-Muslim advisors.

ROLE OF MOSQUES

The mosque was the central institution for the education and improvement of the Muslim community during the time of the Prophet ﷺ and the Rightly Guided Caliphs. Mosques were used for much more than ritual worship. They were used as centres to teach and study the Quran, impart knowledge, explain rules and regulations, hold marriage ceremonies and as courts. The Messenger of Allah ﷺ would give legal judgments inside the mosque and would also meet and entertain visiting guests and dignitaries there.

Today most mosques are quiet, even locked, outside prayer times. Parents and Muslim organisations are guilty of leaving the education and extra-curricular activities to outside un-Islamic forces, resulting in Muslim youth who are openly smoking, drinking, gambling, and fornicating. Mosques need to adopt a much more dynamic role, not only in the Quranic education of the youth but in organising outdoor activities, sports programmes, discussion groups, counselling and advice services, and even nurseries. Reports by educationalists continuously provide evidence that Muslim children in Britain are academically performing below their English, Hindu and Jewish counterparts. Perhaps our mosques could organise evening classes where Muslim undergraduates and teachers could help youngsters with their studies and exam preparations.

The madrasah is often annexed to the mosque and provides a vital function of teaching the Qur'an to children and even adults. The local community should therefore be careful and very choosy about selecting their Imam and teacher. Too often this job is given to overseas Imams who speak little or no English, are unaware of the problems facing Muslim youth in this country, and do not even enjoy their duties. Although students in madrasahs need to learn discipline and to show respect for their teachers and class mates, this is not necessarily achieved by screaming, abuse and physical violence from the teacher. For many children their early memories of beatings and humiliation by their Quranic teachers put them off studying the Quran and Islam for life.

It is also vitally important that children attending the madrasah are taught not only to recite the Quran but to understand its meaning, as well as receiving other Islamic education in accordance with their ages and abilities. It is the duty of the Imam to make such provisions, a fact which indicates the importance of appointing a knowledgeable Imam who is aware of the duties he owes to his community. In history books we read of an incident which took place after the Muslim conquest of Spain. A Christian was passing a madrasah when he noticed that all the young boys studying there had gathered in the courtyard where their elderly Imam was giving them lessons in archery. One of the boys was being dragged by the others through the crowd until he was before the teacher, whereupon the teacher began to beat him. The Christian was disturbed by the harsh beating and rushed to intervene and ask for the reason behind the punishment. The teacher replied simply that the boy in question had refused to join the class in improving their aim in archery, and so he was being punished. The Christian man later wrote about this incident, saying that this incident reflected how the Muslims were managing to conquer and dominate Christian lands everywhere. By teaching their young children the art of warfare and archery, the Muslims were preparing warriors for Islam from an early age.

LOVE OF ALLAH

Introducing children to the love of Allah, fear of His anger, and the desire to be obedient to Him must begin at a young age. It is the parents who, through their own devotion to their Lord, can instil the same devotion in their offspring. A child who receives love and mercy from his parents will be able to appreciate the supreme love and mercy of his Creator. To understand this concept further, let us contemplate the verses of the last Surah of the Quran:

بِسْمِ ٱللَّهِ ٱلرَّحْمَٰنِ ٱلرَّحِيمِ ۞ قُلْ أَعُوذُ بِرَبِّ ٱلنَّاسِ ۞ مَلِكِ ٱلنَّاسِ ۞ إِلَٰهِ ٱلنَّاسِ ۞ مِن شَرِّ ٱلْوَسْوَاسِ ٱلْخَنَّاسِ ۞ ٱلَّذِى يُوَسْوِسُ فِى صُدُورِ ٱلنَّاسِ ۞ مِنَ ٱلْجِنَّةِ وَٱلنَّاسِ

In the name of Allah, Most Beneficent, Most Merciful. "Say: I seek refuge with the Lord of mankind, the Master of mankind, the God of mankind, from the evil of the one who whispers and then withdraws, the one who whispers in the breasts of mankind, from among Jinns and mankind." (Surah al-Nas)

This short Sūrah is one of the most powerful Sūrahs of the Quran, and was recited with Sūrah Al-Falaq by the Prophet ﷺ to ward off Satan, magic and the evil eye from himself and his family. In order to combat the machinations of the devil and his army of satanic cohorts, the Muslim invokes three powerful attributes of Allah: Lord, Master and God. These three attributes reflect exactly the needs of a human being in the three stages of his life: infancy, youth and old age.

The first stage in the life of every person is that of infancy and helplessness. He is born into this world through no will or effort of his own. He is fed, washed, clothed, nursed and carried by his parents. He watches them doing everything for him while he himself is helpless. He knows that his parents will provide for all his needs, from food and clothes to comfort and love. He may even begin to see his father as his rabb, an all-powerful creator and provider. But at the same time he will see his father sitting humbly on the prayer mat with his hands raised in supplication, and he will wonder to whom his father directs his prayers. This is when he is introduced to the fact that Allah is Rabb an-Nās: the Creator and Nourisher of all mankind.

The second stage in the life of man is that of youth and power. He is young, healthy, proud and confident. The young people who roam the streets at night are often fearless, violent and arrogant, especially towards their elders. They wish to be masters, wealthy and feared. Anything that also displays power and opulence will dazzle them, hence their fascination with fast cars and physical prowess. But Allah reminds us all in no uncertain terms that He alone is Mālik an-Nās, Master of all mankind. All power and ability belong to Him alone, despite the peacock-like strutting of today's youth, political leaders and pop stars.

The final stage is that of old age. His hair is grey, he has seen misery and joy, success and failure; he has seen the false promise of eternal youth and agility promised by the world, and now he knows that death is fast approaching. He no longer hankers after youth, power or money, but instead his head is filled with questions about the purpose of life, death and that which awaits him beyond the grave. These are questions which never concerned him during his youth but which begin to concern him increasingly as he grows older. And so the mind of the elderly man may turn to Allah in his quest for answers. He will remember that Allah alone is Ilāh an-Nas, God of mankind.

These three attributes reflect the stages in the life of man, but this does not mean that man should merely appreciate the Power of Allah when he is in his youth, and only worship Him when he is old. The whole of one's life should be devoted to the worship of Allah, not just the twilight years. Death is not the domain of the elderly alone but comes to all ages, suddenly and without warning. Not all people reach old age, and many who do may have spent so much of their lives amassing sins and evil deeds that it becomes second nature to them and amending their ways becomes impossible. Each individual therefore should be introduced to all three attributes of Allah from an early age so that he can worship Him as He deserves and expects to be worshipped. Allah Almighty also says in the Quran,

$$\text{ٱللَّهُ ٱلَّذِى خَلَقَكُم مِّن ضَعْفٍ ثُمَّ جَعَلَ مِنْ بَعْدِ ضَعْفٍ قُوَّةً ثُمَّ}$$

$$\text{جَعَلَ مِنْ بَعْدِ قُوَّةٍ ضَعْفًا وَشَيْبَةً يَخْلُقُ مَا يَشَآءُ وَهُوَ ٱلْعَلِيمُ}$$

$$\text{ٱلْقَدِيرُ}$$

Allah has created you out of weakness, and after that weakness He gave you power, and after that power He gave you weakness and old age; He creates what He wills, for He is the All-Knowing, All-Powerful! (*Sūrah al-Rūm*, 30:54)

This is further evidence of the authority of Allah. During his youthful years a man may become intoxicated by his own power, wealth and abilities, so Allah reminds him of his true reality. He was born naked, vulnerable and helpless, but Allah placed mercy in his mother's heart and she devoted many years to his upbringing. In youth, Allah gives him power and strength, but this cannot last. And in his old age Allah will make him weak and helpless once again. If man was to stop gloating at his momentary youth and strength, and were to reflect on the two weaknesses of old age and infancy, he would have no choice but to admit that the only one worthy of worship is He whose Power never fades, Who is never weak, and Who gives life and takes it away: Allah.

The sensible individual will reflect on this reality and will not allow his personal vanities and success to make him arrogant and tyrannical. He will value his years of health and power as a temporary phase and will use these years to prepare for his old age and inevitable death. Unfortunately most people are not so sensible. They lust after power and wealth in order to oppress and humiliate the weaker people around them.

An amusing story is told about a President of the Soviet Union. He was once travelling in a plane with an entourage of journalists which included a few Muslims. The president was in the mood for ridiculing Islam and mocking the concept of one Supreme God. He turned to the journalists and said that as they believed God lived high above the world, and that as they were at that moment flying high above the clouds, he wished them to show Allah to him. One of the Muslims stood up and said, "Certainly, Sir. Please open the door and step out of the aeroplane. You will meet Allah immediately!"

CHAPTER SEVEN

<u>METHODS OF TARBIYYA (TRAINING)</u>

There are a number of ways in which young children can be trained to follow the path of Islam. Screaming, threats and physical assault are often the most common tactics employed by parents in an effort to discipline their children, but these should be avoided as they achieve little. Children learn to fear rather than love and respect parents who scream and abuse them regularly.

SETTING A GOOD EXAMPLE

'Abdullah bin 'Umar narrated that he was a small boy when the Prophet ﷺ once came to his house. 'Abdullah wanted to play but his mother called him, saying that she had something to give to him. The Prophet ﷺ immediately asked her what she had to give him, and she replied that she had a date in her hand. The Prophet ﷺ then said,

If you had nothing to give him and your only intention was to stop him playing, this would have been written as a lie against you. (Tarbiyyah al-Awlād)

The above incident, though its authenticity may not be established, contains a vital lesson about the evil of lying, even to children[1].

---

[1] The reader may recall here the famous case of one of the Imams of Ḥadīth who travelled a long way to hear a Ḥadīth from a particular person, but immediately returned when he

It is a common practice for parents to demand attention from their children by promising treats, but this promise is not fulfilled. These lies inevitably encourage similar behaviour in children. Parents should not only set the best example possible for their children to emulate, but also remember to hide their own faults. For example, a father who smokes should make it a priority to give up the addiction, but meanwhile he should smoke in secret so that his children do not grow up to imitate him. Research shows that the majority of smokers acquire their habit at a young age from watching adult family members.

A famous story is told of a young boy who used to steal. His first theft was that of a small object, and his mother responded by smiling at him affectionately. The child received encouragement from her behaviour and became braver in his thefts, knowing that his mother would always be pleased to receive the stolen gift. Many years later the young man was involved in a murder and the Qāḍī sentenced him to death by hanging. Just before the punishment was carried out the prisoner was asked if he had any last requests and he replied that he would like to see his mother. His distraught mother went up to him, lamenting and crying, but when she got close to him he leaned forward and bit off her ear. The astounded people asked him to explain his dreadful behaviour and he replied that it was his mother who had led him to the gallows. If she had put a stop to his habit of stealing at a young age, he would never have embarked on the life of crime which was now ending in a hangman's noose.

Parents who regularly pray and recite the Quran will notice that their children will pick up the actions of prayer at a young age. Parents should also make it a habit to recite du'ās aloud so that their children become accustomed to hearing them. The result of this is usually that the children will learn many Du'as without actually being taught to say them. For example, if a mother recites the supplications

---

found the man deceiving his camel with fodder which he did not intend to feed to it, in order to tempt it into its pen.

of going to sleep each time she tucks her children up in bed, they will quickly learn to associate these particular words with bed-time.

TARGHĪB AND TARHĪB (ENCOURAGEMENT AND DETERRENCE)

Targhīb is to tempt someone with rewards, and Tarhīb is to frighten someone with the evil consequences of their bad deeds.

Children need constant praise and rewards as these encourage them to continue whatever they may be doing. So if a child does well in his work at school, the parents should reward him with a present or a treat. If he is committing the Quran to memory, it is a good idea to give him a prize each time he finishes a Juzz'.

Similarly, children should be made aware of the displeasure of their parents when they do wrong. As they grow older they can be told that their bad behaviour is also making Allah Almighty angry with them. For example, the Prophet ﷺ advised the Muslims to teach their children to pray at the age of seven, and to punish them lightly if they were not praying at the age of 10. This Hadith contains much wisdom. It shows that punishment should not be the first option available to parents, as their duty is to teach the children to pray at an early age. This can be very easy if the parents set a good example by praying regularly themselves and taking their children with them to the mosque for prayers. If after many years of good training the child refuses to pray, light physical punishment must then be used.

NAṢĪḤAH (GOOD ADVICE)

The Quran records the beautiful Naṣīḥah given by Luqmān to his son:

وَإِذْ قَالَ لُقْمَٰنُ لِٱبْنِهِۦ وَهُوَ يَعِظُهُۥ يَٰبُنَيَّ لَا تُشْرِكْ بِٱللَّهِ إِنَّ ٱلشِّرْكَ لَظُلْمٌ عَظِيمٌ

Behold, Luqman said to his son by way of instruction, "O my son! Associate not in worship others with Allah, for Shirk is indeed the highest injustice." (*Sūrah Luqmān*, 31:13)

The Prophet ﷺ would also give such Naṣīhah to his Companions regularly. He once said to Ibn 'Abbās,

Guard your duty to Allah and He will guard you. Guard your duty to Allah and you will find Him in front of you. If you ask, ask only from Allah. If seek help, seek help only from Allah. (Tirmidhī)

This attitude of complete trust, dependence and faith in Allah alone in all times of happiness and misery should be inculcated in the child from a very young age.

STORIES, PARABLES AND QUESTIONS

Young Muslim children are often aware of fictional characters such as Goldilocks and Noddy, and these days the Teenage Mutant Turtles, Power Rangers and Teletubbies. But they have little knowledge of Prophets of Allah and the Companions. Parents should tell them stories of the Prophets, feats of valour and Iman of the Companions, the heroic tales of Muslim conquerors and miracles of the Prophets. Books for children are easily accessible these days so there is no room for excuses.

The Prophet ﷺ used to question his Companions with puzzles and parables. He was once sitting with a group of his Companions including some children when he asked them, "*Of all the trees there is one, the leaves of which do not fall, and which is most like a Muslim because all parts of it are beneficial. Which tree is it?"* The Companions began to think of all the trees in the forests but they could not think of the right one. ʿAbdullah bin ʿUmar was a young boy at the time and he guessed that it was the palm tree, but he remained silent out of courtesy for his elders. The Prophet ﷺ then told his Companions that the answer was the date-palm, as its leaves, skin, fruit and even the date-stones are of great benefit to human beings and animals (Bukhārī, Muslim, Tirmidhī & Aḥmad).

This Ḥadīth teaches us the benefit of stories and puzzles, the value of Muslims to their community, and it especially reminds us of the courtesy and respect shown by Muslims to their elders. Not so long ago, children would dare not speak loudly before their parents, they would ask permission before leaving the room, and would stand whenever a teacher walked into the room. The courtesy extended to teachers was such that if a boy was riding his bicycle and he saw his teacher walking, he would not ride past his teacher. Instead he would dismount and walk with his bike until his teacher was out of sight. Today, teachers and parents fear walking past school grounds because of the abusive language they may have to hear. Parents sit quietly and endure the bad behaviour and filthy language of their own children, blaming the schools for not doing their work properly. Yet teaching children respect and courtesy for their elders is the primary responsibility of the family. If parents discharged this duty in a satisfactory manner, the burden on teachers would be lessened considerably.

In 1996 newspapers carried the story of Philip Lawrence, a London school headmaster who was stabbed to death while trying to save one of his pupils from being beaten at the school gates. In the same year more than half a dozen schools hit the headlines because their teachers had been forced to strike in protest at having to teach particularly violent and abusive children, most of them not even teenagers yet. A school in West Yorkshire was forced to close temporarily after some of the teachers were attacked, one of them sexually.

The truth is that these incidents are not isolated cases but represent a growing trend in British society toward violence, hatred for all symbols of authority and contempt for traditional values. These are reflected in the way children openly insult their own parents, students ridicule their teachers and youth throw petrol bombs at the police. It is a fallacy to blame such acts of mindless violence on the technological era in which we live. Each one of these bullies, vandals and hooligans was once a small, innocent child, and his parents must take responsibility for allowing him to deteriorate into a monster.

AFFECTION AND EQUALITY

Children need to be shown a lot of affection from both parents. It is reported that the Prophet ﷺ once said, *"If you have a child then treat him like a child. Play with him like a child and do not impose yourself on him like an adult."* (Ibn ʿAsākir; declared weak by al-Albānī)

The Prophet ﷺ himself showed considerable affection towards children. He once picked up his grandson Ḥasan and kissed him. A Companion called Al-Aqra bin Hābis was watching and commented, "I have ten children and have never kissed them." The Prophet ﷺ replied, *"Allah has removed mercy from your heart"* (Bukhārī, Muslim, Abū Dāwūd, Tirmidhī & Aḥmad).

In another incident the Prophet ﷺ was leading the Fajr prayer, a prayer in which he would usually recite long passages of the Quran. This time he heard a child crying and so cut short his recitation, reading only the shortest Sūrahs of the Quran. During another prayer he was seen carrying his grand-daughter Umāmah, daughter of Zaynab. When he had to go down for Sajdah he would place her on the ground.

As far as possible, children should be given equal love, affection and gifts, as the Prophet ﷺ said, *"Treat your children equally"* (Aḥmad, Abū Dāwūd & Nasāʾī).

It is natural for the youngest child to receive most of his parents' affection, but all children will for some time be the youngest of the family. Parents should be careful not to show preferential treatment to one child over another, as this can cause enmity and rivalry among siblings. It is especially important for parents to beware of preferring sons to daughters. Sadly this is a common practice among many Muslims and must be opposed. In fact it displays a pagan mentality, common to pre-Islamic Arabia but abhorred by the Prophet ﷺ. The Quran treats with contempt the feelings of a pagan father when he hears the news of the birth of a daughter:

وَيَجْعَلُونَ لِلَّهِ ٱلْبَنَٰتِ سُبْحَٰنَهُۥ وَلَهُم مَّا يَشْتَهُونَ ۝ وَإِذَا بُشِّرَ أَحَدُهُم بِٱلْأُنثَىٰ ظَلَّ وَجْهُهُۥ مُسْوَدًّا وَهُوَ كَظِيمٌ ۝ يَتَوَٰرَىٰ مِنَ ٱلْقَوْمِ مِن سُوءِ مَا بُشِّرَ بِهِۦٓ أَيُمْسِكُهُۥ عَلَىٰ هُونٍ أَمْ يَدُسُّهُۥ فِى ٱلتُّرَابِ أَلَا سَآءَ مَا يَحْكُمُونَ ۝ لِلَّذِينَ لَا يُؤْمِنُونَ بِٱلْأَخِرَةِ مَثَلُ ٱلسَّوْءِ وَلِلَّهِ ٱلْمَثَلُ ٱلْأَعْلَىٰ وَهُوَ ٱلْعَزِيزُ ٱلْحَكِيمُ

They assign daughters for Allah - Glory be to Him! But for themselves, whatever they desire! (i.e. sons.) When one of them receives the good news of the birth of a girl, his face darkens and he is filled with inward grief! He hides himself from the people, because of the evil of the good news he received! Will he keep her with dishonour, or bury her in the earth? Certainly, evil is their decision! For those who believe not in the Hereafter is an evil example, and for Allah is the highest example. And He is the Mighty, the Wise.
(*Sūrah an-Naḥl*, 16:57-60)

Another chapter of the Quran begins with the following description of the Day of Judgment:

إِذَا ٱلشَّمْسُ كُوِّرَتْ ۝ وَإِذَا ٱلنُّجُومُ ٱنكَدَرَتْ ۝ وَإِذَا ٱلْجِبَالُ سُيِّرَتْ ۝ وَإِذَا ٱلْعِشَارُ عُطِّلَتْ ۝ وَإِذَا ٱلْوُحُوشُ حُشِرَتْ ۝ وَإِذَا ٱلْبِحَارُ سُجِّرَتْ ۝ وَإِذَا ٱلنُّفُوسُ زُوِّجَتْ ۝ وَإِذَا ٱلْمَوْءُودَةُ سُئِلَتْ ۝ بِأَيِّ ذَنْبٍ قُتِلَتْ ۝ وَإِذَا ٱلصُّحُفُ نُشِرَتْ

When the sun shall be folded up. When the Stars shall fall. When the mountains shall pass away. When the pregnant she-camels shall be neglected. When the wild beasts shall be gathered together. When the seas shall overflow. When the souls shall be joined with their bodies. When the baby girl buried alive shall be questioned, "For what sin was she killed?" (*Surah at-Takwīr*, 81:1-10)

Islam may have abolished pagan practices such as the burying alive of infant daughters, but beliefs in male supremacy have continued in the Muslim world, especially because of the huge impact of Hindu influences. Hinduism converted the belief in the supremacy of men and servility of women into an art-form. The birth of a daughter became an occasion for mourning and her marriage, a burden. Once a woman's husband died, her life was considered to be over and she was obliged to burn herself on his funeral pyre. Muslims today may not bury alive their daughters, but some turn to abortion clinics to kill female foetuses. The birth of baby daughters continues to be treated as a mark of shame, reflected in the fact that many households will distribute sweets when a son is born but nothing when it is a daughter. They forget that Allah Almighty has promised huge rewards for parents who, bring up their daughters with love and affection. The Prophet ﷺ said,

The person who brings up two baby daughters will, after his death, enter paradise with me just as these two fingers of mine are close to each other. (Muslim, Tirmidhī & Aḥmad)

THE ROOTS OF ALL EVIL

The two worst characteristics which a person can possess are arrogance and envy, and most sins and evil deeds can be shown to stem from these characteristics. For example, the first disobedience to Allah was committed out of arrogance, and the first murder on earth took place because of envy. Iblīs was commanded by Allah to prostrate with the angels to Ādam, but he refused due to his own pride. He exclaimed haughtily to Allah,

قَالَ مَا مَنَعَكَ أَلَّا تَسْجُدَ إِذْ أَمَرْتُكَ قَالَ أَنَا۠ خَيْرٌ مِّنْهُ خَلَقْتَنِي مِن نَّارٍ وَخَلَقْتَهُۥ مِن طِينٍ ۞ قَالَ فَٱهْبِطْ مِنْهَا فَمَا يَكُونُ لَكَ أَن تَتَكَبَّرَ فِيهَا فَٱخْرُجْ إِنَّكَ مِنَ ٱلصَّٰغِرِينَ

"I am better than him (Adam)! You created me from fire and You created him from clay." Allah said, "Get down from here, for it is not for you to be arrogant here. Get out, you are among those disgraced!" (*Sūrah al-Aʿrāf*, 7:12-13)

This pride that his origin was better than the origin of Ādam turned Iblīs into the first racist and denier of Allah. The enormity of the sin of pride is such that it transforms humans into devils so that they refuse to acknowledge Allah as their Master and do not bow in worship to Him. Any man who has racist beliefs or refuses to worship Allah is clearly following in the footsteps of Satan and will be punished with him on the Day of Judgment.

The two sons of Adam were told to offer sacrifices to Allah to earn His pleasure. The sacrifice of Habīl was accepted but that of Qabīl was rejected, and so out of envy and anger the latter killed the former. This was the first murder on earth. The same envy caused Prophet Yusuf's brother to throw him into a well and leave him to die. And the same envy caused the Quraysh of Mecca and the Jews of Medina to reject Prophet Muhammad's ﷺ message and to make repeated attempts on his life. In fact the Jews were expecting a final messenger to appear in Arabia and many of them had migrated from surrounding countries to settle in Medina and wait for the promised prophet. But when the honour of prophethood was bestowed upon an Arab and not on a Jew, the envy of the Jews forced them to reject him. The nobles of the Quraysh were similarly envious that their rich ranks had been ignored in favour of a poor orphan, and so they too rejected his prophethood.

IT IS BETTER TO GIVE THAN TO RECEIVE

Children should be encouraged to be generous and charitable from a young age. For example, whenever a child receives pocket-money or gifts of money on occasions like Eid, he should be reminded that there are small children like himself who are poor, starving, orphaned and without homes. He should become accustomed to giving a certain percentage of his money to charity, with the reminder that the money he has parted with will multiply many times in Allah's safekeeping and will buy him a higher status in paradise, *in-shā'Allah*.

Children should also be taught the value of hard work and a Halal income. Today when many governments provide financial help for the poor, too many youngsters who are fit, healthy and able to work choose to sponge off the state in order to laze away their days. They fail to realise that this is equivalent to begging, a demeaning and evil act, and that the best income is that for which a person has worked hard. The story is told of a wealthy merchant who wished to teach his trade to his son. He gave his son some money and sent him off with a caravan of merchants to trade in a distant land. During the long journey the caravan encamped near a forest. The young man noticed an injured fox lying among the trees, unable to move or hunt, and began to wonder how the fox would survive if it could not hunt for food. Soon a lion appeared, dragging its kill in its mouth, and sat down nearby to devour his prey. He left when satiated, leaving the remains of his meal. The fox had been watching quietly and now limped across slowly to the remains of the lion's meal which he happily ate. The young man began to mull over the incident in his mind and concluded that Allah was there to provide food for everyone, even those who did not work for it. "Why should I travel many miles to work hard in a strange land and make some money," he thought to himself, "when Allah can bring the food to my doorstep?" He thus packed his luggage and returned home. His father was surprised to see him back so soon, but when his son had recounted the whole incident to him, he said gravely, "My son, you have learned from the injured fox, but you have not learned from the lion. The lion hunted and so the fox was fed. Be like the lion and earn so that you can feed others. Give to others, and do not expect to receive all the time."

ḤAYĀʾ (MODESTY)

The subject of Haya' is rarely preached and practised even less by Muslims today. Modern society has abandoned any resemblance of decency and modesty, labelling such concepts as Victorian and out-moded. Parents frolic in the semi-nude on beaches with their children watching. Couples cavort together in public un-ashamedly. Parents introduce their young children to the facts of life almost as soon as they are able to talk. Newspapers, magazines, films and television thrive on the sales of pornographic material. Schools encourage children to use contraception, and it is no wonder that recent research has found that more than half of 12 year-olds in Britain have had sexual experiences.

Many of our Muslim families have embraced this lack of modesty in western culture very readily. Subjects which should be strictly private between married couples are discussed openly before children and friends. The birth of a child has become an event for public entertainment, with cameras being present to record the event. This kind of openness is destroying innocence in children and introducing them to adult subjects before their young minds are ready for them. The Prophet ﷺ taught decency, modesty and shame. He once said, "*Modesty is a branch of Faith*" (Bukhārī, Muslim & others).

The Companions used to say about the Prophet ﷺ that he showed more shyness than a young virgin. Parents should thus be very careful about the way they dress and behave in front of their children. They should teach their children to knock before entering their parents' room:

يَٰٓأَيُّهَا ٱلَّذِينَ ءَامَنُوا۟ لِيَسْتَـْٔذِنكُمُ ٱلَّذِينَ مَلَكَتْ أَيْمَٰنُكُمْ وَٱلَّذِينَ لَمْ يَبْلُغُوا۟ ٱلْحُلُمَ مِنكُمْ ثَلَٰثَ مَرَّٰتٍ مِّن قَبْلِ صَلَوٰةِ ٱلْفَجْرِ وَحِينَ تَضَعُونَ ثِيَابَكُم مِّنَ ٱلظَّهِيرَةِ وَمِنْ بَعْدِ صَلَوٰةِ ٱلْعِشَآءِ ثَلَٰثُ عَوْرَٰتٍ لَّكُمْ لَيْسَ عَلَيْكُمْ وَلَا عَلَيْهِمْ جُنَاحٌ بَعْدَهُنَّ طَوَّٰفُونَ عَلَيْكُم بَعْضُكُمْ عَلَىٰ بَعْضٍ كَذَٰلِكَ يُبَيِّنُ ٱللَّهُ لَكُمُ ٱلْءَايَٰتِ وَٱللَّهُ عَلِيمٌ حَكِيمٌ ۝ وَإِذَا بَلَغَ ٱلْأَطْفَٰلُ مِنكُمُ ٱلْحُلُمَ فَلْيَسْتَـْٔذِنُوا۟ كَمَا ٱسْتَـْٔذَنَ ٱلَّذِينَ مِن قَبْلِهِمْ كَذَٰلِكَ يُبَيِّنُ ٱللَّهُ لَكُمْ ءَايَٰتِهِۦ وَٱللَّهُ عَلِيمٌ حَكِيمٌ

O you who believe! Let your slaves and those who have not yet reached the age of puberty ask your permission before entering on three occasions: before the Dawn Prayer, while you put off your clothes for the afternoon rest, and after the Night Prayer. These three times are of privacy for you. Other than these, there is neither sin on you nor them to move about, helping each other. Thus does Allah make the Signs clear to you, and Allah is All-Knowing, Wise. When the children attain puberty, let them also ask for permission, as those senior to them do. Thus does Allah make His Signs

clear to you, and Allah is All-Knowing, Wise. (*Sūrah an-Nūr*, 24:58-59)

The subject of sex education is introduced very early in schools, and parents should make an effort to withdraw their children from these classes until they have reached the age of maturity. It should then be taught within a moral framework and within the context of marriage only. Any sexual acts committed outside a marriage must be explained as adulterous Muslims must take a strong stand for morality, chastity, fidelity and public decency. If we fail, we will be answerable for our apathy and cowardice on two occasions. Once, when we stand in front of Allah and we are asked to justify why we did not speak the truth and oppose the false. But more immediately, we will be answerable to ourselves and our communities when we watch our youth being led astray because we have not established the necessary framework in our schools, homes, mosques and social centres to give them the desperately-needed guidance.

TELEVISION JUNKIES

Muslim teenagers have recently been identified as the largest group of Television Junkies in Britain compared with youngsters of similar ages but from different backgrounds. The study was published in 1996 by Rev. Professor Leslie Francis of the University of Wales, Lampeter and was conducted on nearly 21,000 year nine and year ten pupils. It showed that over 30% of Muslim teenagers watched more than four hours of television daily, compared with 20.7% of Anglicans, 27% of Roman Catholics, 16.1% of Jews, 16% of Hindus and 29.1% of Sikhs. The conclusions of this study should come as worrying news for Muslim parents. Unlike reading books, newspapers and even comics, watching television requires few literary skills. Books extend the reader's literary and creative skills, vocabulary and imagination, in a subtle learning process. Through books the child can wander in a maze of adventures, magical fantasies, historic events and much much more. And unlike television, books require constant and active participation from the reader; the better he reads, the wider his vocabulary and the more active his imagination, the more he will gain from his reading. Reading is not only entertaining and fun but is supremely educational as well.

Television, on the other hand, encourages laziness and passivity. Where books force the reader to read, understand and conjure up the characters and events in his own imagination, television presents everything to the viewer and leaves nothing to the imagination. It has often been said that television has killed off the art of conversation, and we can see the truth of this when we watch our youngsters slumped in front of their TV sets, zapping away with their remote controls at different channels in sullen silence. More and more of children's television is dominated by cartoons and "superhero" characters, and an obsession with mindless violence, superficial dialogue and loud music. Television is also very addictive and children will easily spend many hours slumped lazily in front of it, often at the expense of other beneficial activities such as homework, reading and outdoor sports. To compound the problem, children will switch off their TV sets only to spend a few more hours playing computer games. Not only are these an excellent method of wasting time, but also many signs of ill health have recently been attributed to the electromagnetic radiation from the screens.

Studies have also shown that television addiction in the young encourages violence, anti-social behaviour, laziness and low communication skills. Even more worrying is the attitude of parents who will often allow their youngsters to watch anything on TV, regardless of any pornography, graphic violence or obscene language. Indeed television is often used as a cheap baby-minder by mothers who know their infants will be fascinated by the flickering images and loud noises.

However, the story is not entirely one of doom and gloom. Television is undoubtedly one of the most potent forces in influencing public opinion, imparting information and providing entertainment. If it were not, why else would businesses spend billions on television advertising? It is a powerful yet neutral medium which can be used equally for good or evil purposes, depending on the intentions of the producers and demands by the viewers. It is used to great effect by educational institutions and adds a huge new dimension to the learning process. Programmes about science, nature, travel, world events, geography and many other subjects can convey information to their audience in a thrilling manner. It is thus the duty of parents to be discerning in their choice of television viewing.

Islam is not a boring, dull religion which preaches only worship and abstinence, but a practical code of conduct which permits innocent pleasures and indulgences. We all need to relax and enjoy ourselves regularly and this must not be discouraged if it is achieved through Halal means. Television can offer a feast of educational and entertaining programmes, but these must not become addictive and so time-consuming that the viewer loses all track of time. Parents should also ensure that watching television does not replace other leisure activities which the family enjoy together.

The Muslim community should also not ignore the power of television for disseminating religious information to children and adults alike. Videos on subjects such as the Ḥajj, Tarāwīḥ prayers from Mecca and Islamic lectures have proved to be extremely successful and more need to be produced, especially for children,

It is an undeniable fact that Islamophobia exists and is being nurtured and propagated by the media. The Muslim community may be a victim of prejudice, lies and intolerance, but it should not be a passive victim. We should make our voices heard to prove to the world by our actions and words that we are not a backward, terrorist minority, but a dynamic and global community embracing a wide variety of colourful customs, languages, cuisine and traditions.

The Islamic community cannot be racist, because its creed of the brotherhood and equality of mankind transcends all races. It cannot be cruel and tyrannical, as its creed condemns wrongdoing and promotes justice. It cannot be superstitious because its faith is rooted in the belief and trust in One Supreme God. It cannot be cowardly because its faith teaches valour, self-pride and above all, loyalty to its Creator. It cannot be silent, because it has much to say and teach the world. These messages need to replace the old, regularly revamped stereotypes of the Muslim community, which can only be achieved if we get more positive media exposure. The initiative must come from ourselves.

For this reason the Muslims must be more vocal and active members of their communities, whether it is as parent governors of schools, local councillors, journalists or Members of Parliament. Not only will the Muslims benefit from such active participation but so will the community at large. The values and ethics of Islam encourage hard work, morality, truth, justice, respect for others, care of the elderly, marital loyalty, and above all, love and fear of the Almighty. These are values which need to be conveyed to society at large so that it can stop wandering blindly in the darkness of disbelief

CHAPTER EIGHT

<u>SPARE THE ROD AND SPOIL THE CHILD</u>

Muslims can learn a great deal from the spiralling divorce rates, unruly children and breakdown of family life which are a regular feature of modern homes. This is not to say that we should jump for joy at the misery of others, but that we should learn from their mistakes, take steps to ensure that we do not imitate them, and light a candle so that others too can see their way out of the darkness.

News reports regularly carry frightening stories of criminal activities carried out by mere children, including arson attacks, drug offenses, rape, theft and even murder. In the memories of many Britons remains ingrained the name of James Bulger, the five year old boy who was kidnapped by two 12 year old boys from a shopping centre. They took him to a railway track where they beat him to death with bats, leaving his decapitated body on the railway lines. Philip Lawrence, the headmaster of a London school, was stabbed to death at the gates of his school when he tried to stop a gang of youth beating up one of his pupils. Since his death his widow has been campaigning diligently to bring morality and discipline back into the curriculum of British schools.

Studies into the backgrounds of these juvenile criminals have repeatedly concluded that a common thread runs through them. Whether they came from rich or poor families, educated or illiterate homes, urban or rural communities, they share an upbringing which is severely lacking in discipline, strong morality and decent values.

Schools and parents must take the blame in their failure to provide strict discipline and punishment for bad behaviour. In fact, modern society as a whole shirks its responsibility to punish those who break the laws. Criminals repeatedly walk free from courts, despite their clear guilt, because of insane loopholes in the penal system, clever legal counsel and obvious bullying of jurors. The law goes to great lengths to protect the criminals while doing little for the victims. Even when convicted, criminals are often given sentences so light that they make a mockery of the judicial system.

This failure to provide punishments which are an effective deterrent to crime can be blamed on the legal authorities. But it can also be argued that the State merely reflects the attitudes and values of ordinary citizens. Capital punishment was abolished in Britain because the public and the law-makers decided it was barbaric. If it is re-introduced, it will be because the nation has had enough of the soft approach to crime. Whoever may be to blame, the impact of such laxity is tremendous on children. Youngsters know that they can abuse teachers, bully classmates, rob their neighbours, take drugs, smoke, even insult their own parents, all with clear impunity. Any adult who dares to lay a finger on them, be they teacher, parent or police, will in all probability find themselves being questioned for assault. Untroubled by any feelings of guilt or morality, these youngsters happily embark on their criminal careers.

Strong discipline is also lacking in the homes where parents neglect their responsibility to educate their children in social and moral ethics. Studies have especially isolated homes in which parents are divorced and one parent, often the mother, is doomed to bring up the children alone. Boys who grow up without a father to guide and discipline them will often turn to crime. But discipline and an occasional smack should not mean harsh beatings, bruises and black eyes. Children who experience or witness violence in their homes will treat it as a normal and acceptable part of life, learning to bully and hurt those weaker than themselves.

Another area of concern is that children are not taught to show respect, courtesy and obedience to their elders. When children respond to their parents' efforts at discipline with a barrage of insults, arguments, screaming, stamping of feet and slamming of doors, the parents quietly accept it as "normal". Islam teaches intense respect and obedience to elders, especially parents. The Quran tells us,

وَقَضَىٰ رَبُّكَ أَلَّا تَعْبُدُوٓاْ إِلَّآ إِيَّاهُ وَبِٱلْوَٰلِدَيْنِ إِحْسَٰنًا إِمَّا يَبْلُغَنَّ عِندَكَ ٱلْكِبَرَ أَحَدُهُمَآ أَوْ كِلَاهُمَا فَلَا تَقُل لَّهُمَآ أُفٍّ وَلَا تَنْهَرْهُمَا وَقُل لَّهُمَا قَوْلًا كَرِيمًا

Your Lord has decreed that you worship none but Him, and that you be dutiful to your parents. If one or both of them attains old age in your life, do not say even 'uff' to them (out of disrespect), nor shout at them, but address them in terms of honour. (*Sūrah al-Isrā'*, 17:23)

Obedience and love for parents is such a central tenet of Islam that it is superseded only by submission to Allah. The sacrifices parents make for their children are so many that the children can never repay the debt they owe to their parents.

وَوَصَّيْنَا ٱلْإِنسَٰنَ بِوَٰلِدَيْهِ إِحْسَٰنًا حَمَلَتْهُ أُمُّهُۥ كُرْهًا وَوَضَعَتْهُ كُرْهًا وَحَمْلُهُۥ وَفِصَٰلُهُۥ ثَلَٰثُونَ شَهْرًا حَتَّىٰٓ إِذَا بَلَغَ أَشُدَّهُۥ وَبَلَغَ أَرْبَعِينَ سَنَةً قَالَ رَبِّ أَوْزِعْنِىٓ أَنْ أَشْكُرَ نِعْمَتَكَ ٱلَّتِىٓ أَنْعَمْتَ عَلَىَّ وَعَلَىٰ وَٰلِدَىَّ وَأَنْ أَعْمَلَ صَٰلِحًا تَرْضَىٰهُ وَأَصْلِحْ لِى فِى ذُرِّيَّتِىٓ إِنِّى تُبْتُ إِلَيْكَ وَإِنِّى مِنَ ٱلْمُسْلِمِينَ

We have enjoined on Man to be dutiful and kind to his parents: his mother bears him with hardship, and gives birth to him with hardship. His bearing and weaning is thirty months, till when he attains full strength and reaches forty years, he says, "My Lord! Grant me the ability that I may be grateful for Your Favour which You have bestowed upon me and my parents, and that I

may do good deeds that will please You, and make my offspring good. Truly I have turned to You in repentance, and I am truly of those who submit to You!" (*Sūrah al-Aḥqāf*, 46:15)

Children will not learn such love, devotion and prayers for their parents from thin air, but will have to be taught. Parents must ensure they fulfil this responsibility instead of eternally expecting outside agencies to do their work for them. But it should be remembered that children will never love and obey a parent who shows only anger, hatred and impatience. The key is to teach by good example, which is impossible if the parents themselves have abandoned their aging relatives to old people's homes.

The conclusion we must inevitably reach from observing society around us is that parents must take full responsibility for the behaviour of their children. It is nonsensical to bemoan the friends their children have, the television they watch and the schools they attend. Parents are in a unique position of authority and the manner in which they raise their children will determine the kinds of friends they make and the entertainment they watch. If they see their youth moving towards undesirable company, their response should not be one of quiet acceptance but strong action. Children are born innocent, good and flawless. Whatever they may turn into is a direct result of the society around them, especially their families. Parents should always remember the Prophet's words, *"Every newborn baby is born on the Fitrah (natural state, i.e. Islam). It is his parents who make him into a Jew, a Christian or a Magian"* (Bukhārī, Muslim, Abū Dāwūd, Tirmidhī & others).

وصلى الله على نبينا محمد والحمد لله رب العالمين